Write Yourself a Note

Be confident.
Be great.
Be you!

Holly Hoffman

Be You Holly Hoffman

i

Contents

Write Yourself a Note

Dedication

This book is dedicated to my three amazing children, Austin, Alexandra, and Elizabeth. You three souls are the reason I am the person I am today and why I live my life the way I do. Being a parent is one of the hardest and most rewarding things I have ever done. Watching the three of you grow into fine, independent adults has been my joy and sense of pride for over two decades. Of course, there were times, as a young mother, when I wondered if I was doing things right as a parent — or more often, wondering what I might have been doing wrong. However, watching the three of you take your own paths and grow into successful adults, I know, although I wasn't perfect, that being an active, caring parent paid off. I am so proud of each one of you; and as I dedicate this book, I want you each to know that I love you dearly. Austin, Alexandra and Elizabeth, this book is dedicated to you. I am truly blessed to call you my children.

Write Yourself a Note

Forward by Alex

O n January 5, 2018, our second child was born. Avery Rose was a healthy 10-pound, 13-ounce baby girl. I was diagnosed with gestational diabetes during pregnancy but was otherwise healthy and so was she. Minutes after doctors delivered her via C-section, she went into respiratory distress. I will never forget the sight of doctors and nurses pressing on her little chest trying to help her breathe before rushing her off to the Neonatal Intensive Care Unit. It was the scariest moment of my entire life.

My husband went with Avery as doctors helped her breathe and tried to clear her lungs. They believe she inhaled some amniotic fluid which made it hard for her to breathe on her own. I didn't get to hold my baby girl for 16 hours after she was born. When I finally took her in my arms and looked into her eyes, I promised to be the best mother I possibly could.

The greatest gift my own mother gave to me was

the example she set on how to be a phenomenal mother. I didn't appreciate that fully until becoming a mother myself. Two years prior to the birth of our daughter, we welcomed our firstborn, Jackson, into the world. I will never forget melting into my mother's arms as my parents walked into the hospital room to meet our son, for it was at that moment that I finally understood what being a parent was all about and the sacrifices that my mother had made in her own life for me.

Now, as a parent of two beautiful children, I do everything I can to keep that vow I made to our daughter in the NICU. The lessons my parents taught me and the confidence they instilled in me to face this life are priceless. My mother shares some of those same lessons in the following chapters. Along with that, she shares stories from her own childhood she has never shared with us before. I wept as I read the stories about her abusive, alcoholic father, yet beamed with pride at how she faced and overcame the challenges in her life. After learning more about her childhood, it's easy to see why she is now such an incredible mother.

My mother vowed to give her three children a storybook childhood, and she did. She encouraged us to pursue our dreams, she was always that smiling face in the crowd at sporting events or extracurricular activities, she gave us a shoulder to lean on when we needed it, and most importantly, she shaped who we are today. She was, and still is, our rock. No matter what stage of life you are in now, no matter what challenges or difficulties you may face, I hope the following pages bring you as much comfort and peace as they have given me my entire life.

Write Yourself a Note

Forward by Austin

I am privileged to be the only son of an amazing and strong woman. A woman who not only had the courage and insight to transform her own life into one of meaning, but also the passion and inspiration to share her success and struggles for the betterment of others. I couldn't be prouder of my mother for writing this book, and honestly, I'm surprised she didn't do it sooner. The reason why I feel that way is simple. It is because she is a living, breathing example of *Write Yourself a Note*. She embraces change, surrounds herself with good people, is appreciative of the opportunities that have presented themselves in her life, and is always moving forward and embracing the NOW. This book is second nature to her being and the way she lives her life.

Like most, I wasn't a model child and certainly made my fair share of mistakes. Over the years, my mother has fought for me, with me, and even against me at times where I needed a hard dose of reality. I wasn't always grateful for her honesty or proverbial kick in the pants when I was deserving. However, no matter the circumstance, I know that she has always treated me fairly, had my best interest in mind, and has never wavered in her support of me to be the best human I can be.

Not many people know this, but shortly after I turned 21, I wanted to drop out of college and give up my dream of being a lawyer to move home, sit in a tractor all day, and work cattle. Now, there is nothing wrong with sitting in a tractor or working cattle. Some of the best and brightest people I know do just that. However, my mother was unyielding in her belief that until I was fully educated with a four-year degree under my belt, I wasn't equipped to make a life-changing decision that would alter the path of my life indefinitely. It was a conversation I'll never forget and a humbling one to say the least. However, it is exactly what I needed to hear and changed the course of the rest of my life. Since that time, I finished my degree, moved back to our hometown, and opened my own law practice. I have two wonderful boys, Cohen and Theo, and a wife, Megan, who deserves sainthood. Sitting in a tractor and working cattle is still something I'll enjoy later in life, but it will have to wait until the time is right. It is my hope that I will be half the parent to my children as my mother has been, and is, to me. I am grateful every day for her love, support, and wisdom, and I am so happy she has decided to share her positive insight on the world, with the world.

I know you are going to love this book as much as I do and have no doubt that if you practice the principles presented here on a regular basis, you will live a happier, fulfilled, and enlightened life. So, what are you waiting for? Start reading and don't stop until you have finished.

Write Yourself a Note

Introduction

I've been blessed to travel the United States giving motivational speeches and delivering presentations. I offer my own brand of encouragement and optimism to people in all stages of life, no matter their demographic or life status. Although I didn't fully appreciate it until later in life, after my experience on *Survivor*, I recognized the power of self-motivation, happiness, and focused change. In my heart, I truly believe each of us has the ability to focus our thoughts, emotions, and energy toward success.

After *Survivor*, I was awakened, and my personal journey evolved into a life that included opening myself up to strangers for the purpose of giving their lives more meaning, and through the process of doing so, I've bettered my own life. Throughout my travels, I have met some amazing people! These are people who inspire ME to be a better person each day and to never stop growing emotionally and intellectually. When I'm weary from travel and wonder if I'm doing too much or too little in the world, I think about my purpose: inspiring, mentoring, learning, listening, and being grateful every day. Nothing pleases me more than when others take the time to share their stories, hopes, and dreams with me.

I started to realize how so many of us get caught up in the hustle of our daily lives that we lose the knowledge, tools, and discipline to maintain focus on our higher priorities – myself included. At the end of the day, unless I made a conscious effort to bring myself back to center and refocus, I found that often I was just getting through the day to start the next one. That is not the way I want to live my life. This desire to live focused every day was my inspiration for *Write Yourself a Note* – both the speech and this book. I wanted to give people a simple tool they can rely on every day to refocus and reprioritize. In this book, I offer encouragement, optimism, and a road map for self-discovery. I hope you find my methods — the ones I use every day in my own life — intuitive, honest, and adaptable to nearly any individual or situation. My goal for this book is to inspire you to consistently work towards a successful and fulfilling life for yourself.

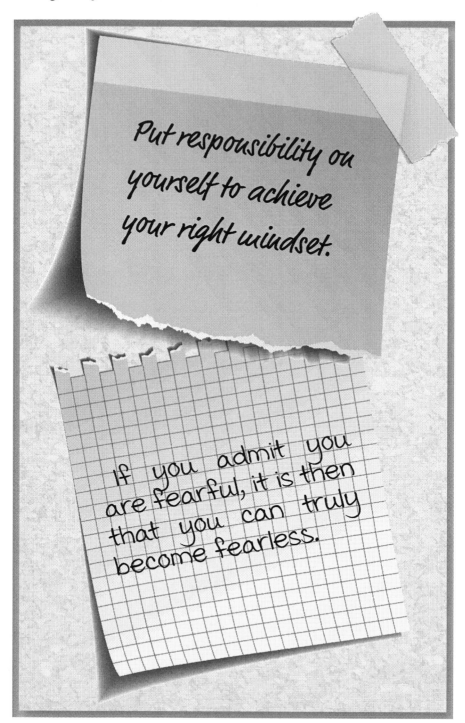

Put responsibility on yourself to achieve your right mindset.

If you admit you are fearful, it is then that you can truly become fearless.

Say yes to opportunities by first saying yes to yourself.

Write Yourself a Note

CHAPTER 1

Opportunities Create Happiness and Eliminate Fear

Never pass up an opportunity. Make the conscious decision to accept all opportunities. We have all heard those two phrases before. However, we tend to hold ourselves back from opportunities that come our way for lots of reasons. Many times, we use excuses; I don't have time, there is no way I can do that, or, this is not the right time in my life. We convince ourselves we cannot accept the opportunity ahead of us.

Personally, I have accepted many opportunities in my life. One was the hardest thing I have ever done in my life. This particular opportunity became a challenge, because I was faced with fear. It is in those times in our lives that we are challenged and become fearful that prove to be the most rewarding. It is in those times that we find out what our true survival skills are. This particular challenge made me realize that there is no challenge more challenging or rewarding than the challenge to improve yourself.

You're probably wondering, what is this "big challenge?" Well, I applied to be on the reality show, *Survivor*. This opportunity forced me to step out of my comfort zone. It challenged me both physically and mentally. However, it proved to be one of the most rewarding adventures I have ever embarked on.

I have always been one to encourage others to accept opportunities; but sometimes, we encourage others while holding ourselves back from stepping outside of our own comfort zone. I am certain most of you can think of many reasons why you have held yourself back from opportunities that have come your way. In life, we have one shot at most of the opportunities that life offers us; and if we don't at least try, we will never know how our lives may have changed for the better. Sometimes, you have to convince yourself instead of relying on others to do it for you. Put the responsibility on yourself — it is all achievable with the right personal mindset! Never hold yourself back; because in life, we already have too many other people doing that for us.

One of the biggest challenges that hold us back from accepting opportunities is fear of the unknown. How many times do we sign up for something and then the closer we get, we become extremely fearful and focus on the things that could go wrong instead of focusing on all of the things that could go right? When we are in situations that cause us to fear the unknown, particularly in situations that involve security, it may trigger survival skills that we never thought we had. Even positive situations can be fearful: getting married, having a baby, or starting a new job. Making changes is hard, especially when the consequences of those changes are yet unknown.

The first thing you must do is admit that you are afraid. Everyone is afraid of something. I am; you are; everyone is. If you admit that you are fearful, it is then that you can truly become fearless. And most often, you are not alone in the things that you fear. For example, most people are afraid of creepy, crawly snakes, spiders, and bugs. There is no need to feel embarrassed! Feeling embarrassed and not admitting the things you are fearful of will not help you to overcome them. Admit what scares you; journal what you are fearful of. You cannot let fear control you, and writing it down is the first step.

You can then visualize it on paper. This is the first step. Look at it over and over again, and make a simple note to yourself that you can face this fear.

I am fearful of many things; and as a child, I was very fearful of water. I remember our family being at a hotel for a family wedding, and everyone was in the swimming pool. Even with a life jacket on, I would not get off the steps. My brothers, cousins, parents, aunts, and uncles all tried to convince me that I would not drown with a life jacket on; but I just could not put my trust in that life jacket. I could not even put my trust in them and what they were telling me. Even though I was able to watch everyone swim around with life jackets holding him or her up, I was still convinced that somehow the life jacket would not work for me.

Fear is a strange thing. It can mess with your mind to the point of convincing yourself that you cannot overcome whatever it is you're fearful of. In the situation I described above, I visualized others staying above the water with their life jackets on, but I could not convince myself to even try to swim with one on. I was not able to face my fear. I needed to admit to myself that I was fearful and to face my fear in order to become fearless. I never did get off those steps that day. I never jumped into that water. However, as I got older and finally faced my fear of swimming, I put my trust in the life jacket. Eventually, I was even able to swim without one. I had to take the first step of admitting my fear; it was only then that I was able to overcome it.

Facing your fears starts with admitting what you're fearful of. That is the first step. As I look back to that situation, I now realize the only person who was holding me back from jumping into the swimming pool that day was myself. I was holding myself back, but it's amazing how great life can be when you just face your fears and trust in life's life jackets.

Now, I don't mean to say that we all must be these fearless beings who have no fear of absolutely anything. If that were the case, we surely wouldn't survive very long in today's world. We would be walking into oncoming traffic, stepping off the rooftops, and maybe even handling poisonous snakes. When it comes to true survival skills, it's okay to be fearful and use one's common sense. Fear promotes survival. For me, I do not care how many times I write down I'm scared of snakes — because when I see a snake (no matter how big or small!), I will run and scream! I am convinced I may never overcome the fear of snakes. And, when it comes to survival, that might not be a bad thing. I will run away from garter snakes for the rest of my life; because someday, it may just be a rattlesnake.

Now, you've admitted you're afraid. You've taken the first step. What's next? The second step is to focus on your success. You may have been fired from a job, and the fear when taking a new position is that you'll be fired again. However, don't focus on that job! Focus on how you are going to become better at your next job. Face the fear of being fired, and find the successful career you've always wanted. Do not fear failure so much that you let it hold you back from the opportunity to become successful.

For example, I was asked to speak about my experience on *Survivor* after I returned from the show. I was so fearful of being up on a stage in front of people speaking that I feared I would not be able to do it. Sometimes, I still feel like I'm going to pass out! However, I face that fear in order to have a successful career as a professional motivation speaker. I have learned to look out over the audience and focus on the people who are smiling, clapping, and nodding their heads in agreement with what I am saying. When I have those moments where I am fearful and feel like I am going to pass out, I recognize my fear, face it, and focus on previous success. I focus on the last time I got a standing ovation or when someone gave me a hug after a powerful speech. I face my fear, which is getting up in front of people, and I focus on the success. These first two steps allow us to let go of the fear of the unknown and not focus on the failures, but rather the successes. Success really does help to eliminate fear.

Admitting your fears and focusing on your success are the first two steps. The third step is simple: don't look back. We tend to continue to look back on situations and moments when we were overcome with fear. However, doing this only makes us face that fear again and again. I encourage you to look at the situation in a way that you don't continually look back at fear, rather you reflect on it, learn from it, and move forward. As you move forward, you need to encourage yourself to be accountable, consistent, and prepared. Take life one day at a time. In my career, when I walk off the stage and focus on what I said and did well, rather than focusing on what I forgot to say, I feel successful. When I focus on the negative and look back on what I did poorly, I'm not focusing on the step. I'm looking back to fear, which just makes things worse; because then you're neglecting step two of the process, which is focusing on success. Yes, I miss stuff. Yes, I stumble. But it's when you stumble that you need to get up and move forward. Look forward to what's ahead — to better opportunities and to self-improvement. Too many of us in our lives continue to look back on what we should have done in the past. We focus on failure instead of looking forward to find success. Don't be one of those people who continue to reflect back on their failures. Don't be one of those people who forget that success is ahead of you; you are not defined by what lies behind you.

In summary, by admitting your fears, focusing on success, and never looking back, you will have the strength and ability to accept and conquer every opportunity that comes your way. Say yes to opportunities by first saying yes to yourself. If you are negative to yourself, you are limiting your options. Sure, accepting opportunities can be risky; but if you never try, you will never know. Opportunities force you to step outside of your comfort zone. This is a space where your activities and behaviors fit a routine and pattern that is not stressful and is of no risk. You have a sense of familiarity and security inside your comfort zone. You focus on the idea that stepping outside of your comfort zone is a risk that causes you to feel stressed and anxious. You start asking questioning yourself and wonder what will happen and how you will adapt to the change. But, within your comfort zone, there is little stress. We all have stress in our lives but considerable more stress when we step out beyond ourselves. By staying in your comfort zone, you can be consistent and possibly in control of situational outcomes. By stepping out of your comfort zone and into a new challenge, you take that risk of fear setting in. However, the risk can also be one of the best opportunities you have ever taken, and it can give you something you never had — it can even give you a profound sense of happiness. I do believe that opportunities have the potential to create happiness. It is always possible, of course, to make the wrong decision about an opportunity; but the wrong decision is still better than never taking a chance in the first place. When it comes to an opportunity, make the decision to say yes, because that one opportunity may change your life. That one opportunity may help you face your fears. That one opportunity may just bring you a sense of happiness you never thought you could have.

As humans, we are creatures of comfort. We like what we know and understand. We don't like change and having to adapt. Our comfort zone provides us with just that: comfort. Stress and anxiety are minimal. There is nothing wrong with staying within one's comfort zone, but I encourage you to never get too comfortable and hold yourself back from new opportunities. You'll end up in this "safe place" where you don't try new things, you're not challenged, and you don't grow as a person. Step out of your comfort zone and discover your survival skills. You never know where that one opportunity is going to take you. Maybe it'll lead you into a swimming pool where you will learn to swim, to a stage you never thought you could stand on, or maybe even find happiness that you never thought was possible. So I encourage you, do three things: admit your fears, focus on the successes, and never look back. And it all starts with writing yourself a simple note.

As you finish each chapter, you are going to use the space provided to write yourself a note. Let's face it — most of us are list people. We make lists ABOUT lists! I sometimes have a list on my desk, a list on the refrigerator, a list in my car, a list in my purse... well, you get the idea. But what are those lists or notes even about? They are usually about the things we need to get done. The "to-do" lists: get the groceries, do the laundry, pick the kids up from soccer practice, plan a birthday party, meet a friend for dinner, call someone, etc. But how many of us make a "to-do" list for ourselves? How many of us make a list of the things we can do to improve ourselves? I encourage you throughout this book, to open yourself up to the opportunity to grow as a person and to remind yourself daily about the things you can do and work on. As you write yourself a note, think about an opportunity that you would like to take. What is holding you back? How can you make it happen? This is YOUR note to yourself – nobody else but you. It's time for you to think about you.

As you do this, after each chapter, think about what the focus was on that chapter and write your note accordingly. Take a few seconds, take a few minutes, take a couple hours, but make sure your note to yourself is for you and only you.

In case you want examples, I'll provide some before each exercise. I did a presentation in Anaheim, California; and after I was done speaking,

I asked the ladies in the audience to write them-selves a note. I am honored to share some of their notes with you in my book.

Noteworthy Notes

✏️ **Amber from California wrote herself a note:**

"Don't be afraid of the unknown; dare to do the things that truly make you happy, even if they are scary."

✏️ **Laurie from Utah wrote herself a note:**

"I have worth. I will believe in myself. I do matter."

✏️ **Michaelann from Chicago wrote herself a note:**

"I am going to 'ask' more."

Write a note to yourself about an opportunity that you want to take. It's YOU time!

_____

_____

_____

_____

_____

_____

_____

_____

_____

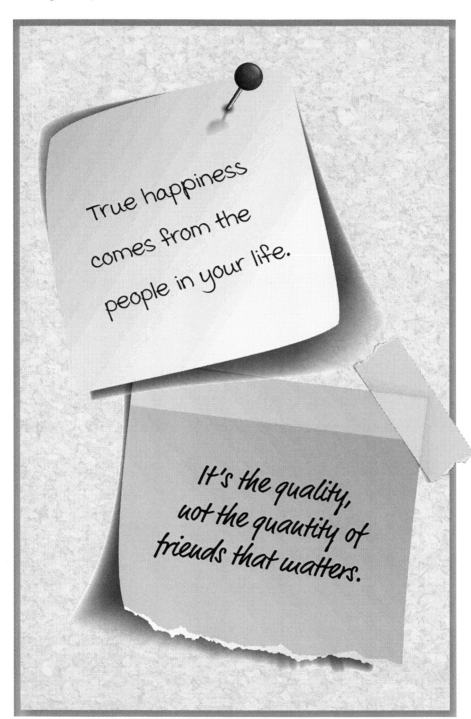

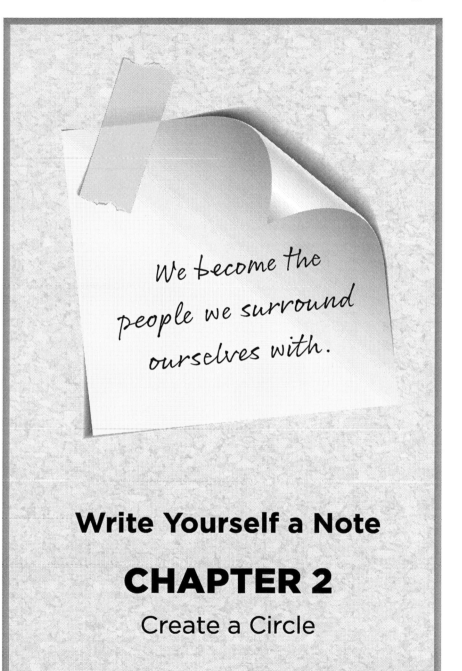

We become the people we surround ourselves with.

Write Yourself a Note

CHAPTER 2

Create a Circle

Growing up, I did not have the easiest childhood. My parents divorced when I was in the sixth grade, and that definitely took a toll on me. I always felt I had a hard time fitting in, and I was always worried that I wasn't smart enough, I wasn't social enough, and I wasn't pretty enough. I never showed these insecurities on the outside, but they were always there. However, this is where "my circle" came in. My circle of friends was not very big, but they were powerful. I had a group of people who supported me through good times and bad. For me, I found that it was the people I surrounded myself with who truly helped me through my childhood; and to this day, I have a group of people who I rely on through the good times and the bad. I believe it's not how big your circle is, but how powerful. It's the quality of the friendships that truly matters.

What I have realized over time, and what was made even more evident during my time on the reality show *Survivor*, is that our success in life has a lot to do with the people we choose to spend our time with. How smart are you? How social are you? How beautiful are you? What kind of family environment did you grow up in? Is that what's important? Now, don't get me wrong; for a lot of people, all of these aspects are very important. I just believe that it's more important to have a group of people to support you through life's journey. People to laugh with, and people to cry with. It's the people you surround yourself with, the people in "your circle" that really matter.

An individual can have all of the riches in the world and, yet, still be unhappy. True happiness comes from the people in your life. The people you surround yourself with influence your way of thinking, they influence your behavior, and they help form your mindset. You need to be careful what type of people you pick in order to create a mindset of success. If you want to be happy, find happy people to be around. If you want to be successful, surround yourself with successful people. If you want to be confident, surround yourself with those who are confident. In short, we become the people we surround ourselves with. We lift ourselves up to their level, because we create a circle of support and love with those people.

What does your circle look like? Is your circle supporting you? How are you working on creating your circle? It's very simple: spend time with family and friends, and find people who uplift you and help you accomplish your dreams. Most people need and want friends. As life gets busy, we sometimes forget to reach out to our loved ones. However, I encourage you to take five minutes and write them a letter, send them an email, or call them on the phone. Let your loved ones know you love them, and you are thinking about them.

I also encourage you to accept those in your circle for who they are. Respect them. Trust them. We all change and grow in our lives, and having supporting family and friends will allow your relationships to foster over time and grow and change as you do. If those in your circle refuse to grow with you, if they refuse to support you in your endeavors, perhaps you need to think a little harder about why you chose them to be an integral part of your life. Growth is about change. Since I started speaking, I have had to do a lot of traveling. It has been a change for many of the people in my circle. But my true friends and family are the ones who have continued to support me and guide me along the way. Those are the family and friends who have continued to reach out to me, who have been there through my ups and downs, and who have helped me to become successful. You should have people in your circle who support you, but remember that you are also part of your circle and you help keep the circle together. Without your own confidence and determination, and without your own effort to reach out and communicate, your circle may become broken. It may become broken and form a line — which keeps going but is not connected; whereas, a circle is connected forever. That connection is what forms a really solid support system and provides you with guidance, so it is important to keep that circle together.

Society has a tendency to focus on romantic relationships as being of utmost importance; and yes, it's okay for that to be a part of your circle. But I also truly believe that friends and family are important. True friendships and a supportive family can help to improve your mood, help you reach your goals, support you through hard times, support you as you age, and help keep your circle connected. I once met a young lady who told me she likes to be alone. She told me she hates being around people. I tried to explain to her that wasn't healthy. As our conversation continued, we finally got to the core of the problem. She was not happy with herself. She did not want to be around people and make friends, because she did not like the person she was. She didn't really have a circle of friends, because she failed to try. As the years went by, she became more outgoing because she took better care of herself. She became more confident in who she was. Looking in the mirror and liking the person who reflects back at you is an integral part of creating a solid circle. You have to love yourself to make that circle complete. Make yourself a part of your circle.

As I mentioned earlier, my childhood wasn't always easy for me, and I sometimes felt like my circle was a line — and at times even seemed to be a very broken and jagged line. My true circle wasn't discovered in my life until I took an opportunity to be on *Survivor* and I stepped outside of my comfort zone. I discovered that I could do things I never even imagined. I discovered the importance of surrounding myself with people who uplifted me, supported me, guided me, and who made the effort to continue to be a part of my life. Create your personal circle with dignity and pride. Be selective in who you choose. Your circle is an essential part of who you are and an important part of your life journey. Keep your circle close to your heart; they are the people who will support you through the good times and the bad. Keep your circle connected; don't let it turn into a line. Choose your circle wisely!

As you think about the people that are part of your circle, it is time for you to write yourself a note. *Write Yourself a Note* about the importance of your circle. Who do you have in your circle? Why are they such an important part of your life? Think about the qualities you admire in relationships. Write yourself a note, and take a look at that note daily to remind yourself of the people you are surrounding yourself with.

Write Yourself a Note

Noteworthy Notes

 Heather from Maine wrote herself a note:

"Never let the naysayers bring you down and tell you that it can't be done."

 Diane from Texas wrote herself a note:

"Focus on finding happiness in myself."

 Mardi from Ohio wrote herself a note:

"I am going to work on my listening skills."

Write a note to yourself about the importance of your circle and the people in it.

_____

_____

_____

_____

_____

_____

_____

_____

_____

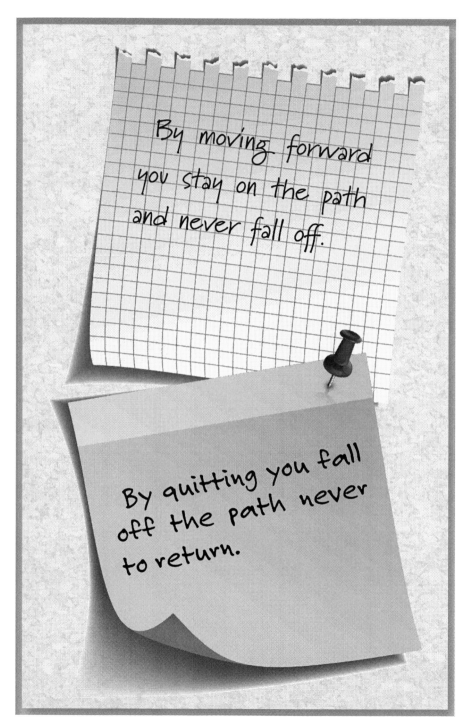

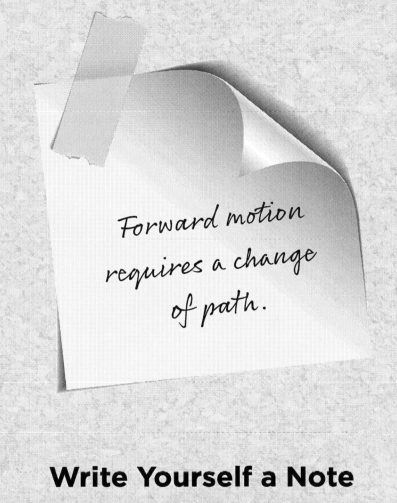

Forward motion requires a change of path.

Write Yourself a Note

CHAPTER 3

The Difference Between Giving Up and Moving Forward

Have you ever been moving forward in your life, and yet feel like you were giving up on something? You may feel like moving forward and not continuing to pursue something you have been working on, which is the same thing as quitting. However, there is a huge difference between giving up and moving forward. Nobody wants to quit things and be labeled a quitter. Quitting is one of the easiest things you can do in life. However, moving forward and pursuing different avenues of success may be one of the most rewarding things you will ever do. When you move forward, you're not quitting or giving up; you are just changing your path to success. Forward motion requires a change of path. Just because you do not want to continue down the same path you've been on, and you need to take a different direction, it doesn't mean you are a quitter. Quitting is falling off of the path entirely without any plan for returning.

For some, this concept is confusing, because what's the difference between quitting something and moving forward? Well, giving up is dropping something entirely, because it's pushing you out of your comfort zone. People usually give up entirely when things get too hard, when they've felt like they've failed over and over again, or when the task at hand is just too much work. But, when you move forward, you are improving yourself or your situation but just changing the course of your path.

For example, at one point in my life, my mother was in a very toxic relationship with my father. My father was an abusive alcoholic, and my brothers and I never knew what the situation would be at home. For part of my childhood, I was raised with a sense of fear and uncertainty. My mother needed to move forward, but she didn't want to be labeled as a quitter. However, she wasn't giving up on my father. In fact, she tried many times to help him improve his own life — but he wanted nothing to do with it. When she decided to divorce my father, she was staying on the path of being a good mother and providing for her children. She knew she needed to change the course of her path in order to do this. The direction of her life, and her children's, was going to improve. She didn't give up on her marriage; rather, she fought to improve the lives of her children and her own.

Moving forward can cause heartache. It can cause loneliness. But at the same time, the end result can be extremely rewarding and joyful. If your path needs to be changed because of a toxic relationship, or a relationship you no longer feel is founded in happiness and love, ask yourself this one question: "Will I let one person or situation cause me to abandon love altogether? (Which would be quitting!) Or can I let that person go while still keeping the possibility of loving another in my heart? (That's moving forward!)"

Another example for you: When I was a freshmen in high school, I made the varsity girls basketball team. Because I was only a freshman, some of the juniors and seniors became envious of a freshman taking their spot. They started mistreating me. I started to feel like I was more of a burden to the team than anything else. I told the coach I was going to quit. I handed my uniform in and told him I wasn't fitting in, and I just couldn't play. He convinced me to stay on the team and encouraged me to continue to work on fostering relationships with the upper classmen. I remember him telling me that sometimes life is going to be hard. He told me that, if I set a precedent of being a quitter now, I would be setting myself up for a lot of failure in life. I think about this often. Every time something gets hard, don't just quit. Move forward. I decided to stay on that basketball team. I chose to continue to improve my game for the team. Yes, it was hard. I still felt it was hard to foster relationships and gain trust. There was jealousy and envy rooted in the situation, but I am glad I was encouraged not to quit just because of that. I went from wanting to quit, to changing my direction, and moving forward.

In terms of a career, I'm sure we've all had a job where we showed up every single day and wanted to quit. It may have been a job that started out perfect but then became stressful and wasn't what we expected at all. When you talked to people about it, perhaps they encouraged you to continue working and not give up. However, having a job that makes going to work miserable every single day with constant thoughts of quitting is not the ideal career. Knowing when it's time to move forward to a different job is not quitting. You're not leaving because the work is too hard, the hours are too long, or you have no coworkers you enjoy. You're leaving because you need something that better suits your abilities and your goals for your own personal career. You may even want to change your career path, and the job you have is not what you want for your life. Maybe the work environment is toxic and leaves you without satisfaction, stressed and unhappy.

When I was in the sixth grade, my parents were recently divorced, and I knew it was time for me to get a job. I needed to help my mother out; and if I worked in the summertime, I could buy all my own school supplies and school clothes. I applied at the local drive-in, and I was so excited when I got the job. The day I started, I was extremely nervous. I hoped I could do everything right and catch on to all the new skills the job required. Believe me, the first few ice cream cones I made were pretty much a disaster! However, with some practice and a little wasted ice cream, they soon started to improve. Waiting on customers, I was also so nervous. I wanted to get everything right with their order. I focused on perfection and really worked hard to satisfy the customers. However, in my heart, I felt I couldn't do anything right. The first day, I couldn't satisfy the boss. He wasn't happy with my work and expected more from me than I felt I could give. I remember going home crying and telling my mother I thought I was going to quit. I gave it a few more weeks and a little more thought, and it continued the same. I worked hard, the boss wasn't satisfied, and I left feeling awful. I ended up leaving that job and moved forward to something better. I found another job that same summer at a local clothing store, and I loved it! I was passionate about working with the customers. I worked hard and had a better relationship with my boss. That job taught me the value of communication, and hard work, and probably taught me to love shopping a little too much. By letting go of my first job and finding another, I veered on a little different path and was able to move forward and find success. Had I left the first job and given up on ever finding another, that would have labeled me as a true quitter. But sometimes, you have to switch paths to find success.

Think of a situation in your life where you feel you quit, and a situation in your life where you felt you have moved forward. Can you compare the difference? By moving forward, you stay on the path and you never fall off. By quitting, you fall off the path never to return.

And now it's time, again, to write yourself a note. Think about your career goals in your life. Think about your happiness and your career. What do you love about it? Where can you improve? Do you wake up every morning excited to go to work, or do you dread the day and are looking to move forward? Write yourself a note about where you are in your career and whether you're happy there or want to be on a different path.

Noteworthy Notes

 Mary from California wrote herself a note:

"Become a certified personal trainer within one year — for women — before my 60th."

 Barbara from Kansas City wrote herself a note:

"Become a model for positivity."

Write a note to yourself about where you are in your career, and if you're happy or want to move forward on a different path.

_____

_____

_____

_____

_____

_____

_____

_____

_____

_____

When taking steps to change always be flexible.

Show change — don't just speak it.

Change is about letting go of the familiar.

Write Yourself a Note

CHAPTER 4

Transition to Change

Change. It's something we are all faced with. The worst thing about change is when it's unexpected. Most of us like to feel like we have some sort of grip on our lives. We have a sense of what we are doing next, where we are going, and how are we feeling. And mostly, we feel in control. Unfortunately, it's not always like that. Change happens every day. Sometimes expected; sometimes unexpected.

For example, imagine you are driving to work and run into a major construction project, and you have to take a different route to work. How does that make you feel? If you are already running late, it's likely you feel a combination of stress, tension, anger, confusion, and overall just uncomfortable. Who do we take all those emotions out on? Perhaps, we honk our car horn; maybe we give a dirty look here and there. Maybe we call a loved one and vent about how we're going be late to work, and we are sick of constant construction. This is because change scares us, and we feel out of control. This is when we need to take a breath and look at the transition of change. Change and transition are a natural part of life. When you experience change and transition in life, you are letting go of what is familiar to you and moving forward with what is unfamiliar. Change is about letting go of the familiar.

Change can be stressful, regardless of whether it is positive or negative, whether it is planned or unexpected. You need to recognize the change you need to make. People can tell you over and over again that you need to change; but unless you take their advice, you will never see the change you need to make. YOU are the one that needs to make the change. Embrace humility, take their advice, and put their advice into action. There's a big difference between talking about doing something and actually doing it. You can "talk the talk" over and over, but you need to "walk the walk" to make it happen.

The first step to change is recognizing the change you need to make. Sometimes that is very hard, because who wants to admit they need to change? Nobody wants to admit they're wrong or they need to change, so use your best judgment to change. Utilize the ones you trust in your circle. Recognize that change needs to happen. Recognition is your first step, and you need to be sure you're making that change for yourself and not for anybody else.

The second step is to take small steps toward change. Do not expect it to just happen overnight. You cannot always control what happens next on your journey, but you can work on having more control of your reaction to what happens as well as your outlook on new changes and transitions. When taking small steps toward change, always remember to be flexible. Although life doesn't always unfold the way you planned, you must learn to recognize the small steps you need to take and put those small steps into action. We have all heard the staying "actions speak louder than words," so start your small steps of action. Showing is believing. Show someone you're making change, because something someone is actually doing is going to be more powerful than merely speaking about it. Show change — don't just speak it. As you take small steps, you also need to focus on the finish line. Set a goal for yourself. Make the goal realistic. And take small steps of change with the goal in mind.

The third step is to not revert back to where you came from. When we begin to realize we need to change, many times we ask ourselves "what if," when we should be asking ourselves "why not!?" Stay positive! Staying positive and moving forward is about not looking back. It's easy to go back to the familiar, but true change requires us to step outside of our comfort zone and focus on the ultimate goal.

When my mother made the decision to move forward, she was about to make a big change. She had $7.35 in her bank account when she divorced my father. She was raising three children and needed to keep moving forward to survive. The biggest change she made was going from a stay-at-home mom to having to find three jobs to put food on the table for her three children. The change she made was huge. She made the decision in order to better herself and her children. When she realized a change needed to be made, she didn't look back. There was only one direction to go and that was forward. Did we still struggle? Yes. Many nights, we had a bowl of cereal for dinner. But my mother always worked hard to provide for us, and she always loved us and cared for us. She made so many changes for my brothers and me. We did not have very much growing up, but we had each other. We made up our "circle," and that circle was tighter than ever. My mother was strong and fearless, and she was the core of our circle. When you're facing a change, it is so important to keep your circle strong.

The fourth step of change is putting the change into action. Change requires action. We can think about change, but how do we actually initiate it? We need to be accountable. Accountability is a ma-

jor step to change. The best way to be accountable is to rely on others for help; and for most of
us, asking for help can be extremely hard and very
humbling. But, there are times in our lives when we
must ask for help. Most of us have a mindset that
we can do it all. But really, we can't. And we need
to realize it is okay to ask for help. Imagine that
change is like a building a house. You've got to accomplish each task well enough to support the next
step. If you don't get the foundation right, the house
is not going to be sturdy, and it will eventually fall
apart. Get other people involved to help you stay
accountable! Formulate a plan of action! By having
a plan and getting others involved, you will be accountable. Surrounding yourself with positive people can really help you with this step. If you want to
get into shape and cannot get yourself out of bed
in the morning to workout, find a workout partner
to hold you accountable. That way, you can make
a plan to workout together. Make sure the people
who you choose are going to help lift you up and
not put you down. In short, put your change into
action and keep moving on to where you want to
be. Set a goal and take small steps toward reaching
that goal. When you change your typical pattern of
living, you truly can change your life

Before discussing the fifth and final step, let's
briefly review. The first few steps are to recognize
the change you need to make, taking small steps
towards change, not to reverting back to old habits,
and putting the change into action. All the steps
allow you to move towards successfully changing whatever aspect of your life you've chosen.
Finally, the fifth and final step is reinforcement.

Have you ever met someone who made a huge change to lose weight, they started dropping off pounds, and they looked great! They had to change their habits and their lifestyle. Then, once they reached their goal, they started reverting back to old habits. We must continually reinforce change in order to make it permanent. One of the best ways to have reinforcement is to write yourself a note. You can remind yourself daily of the bad habits you have removed from your life and the improvements you have made. You can congratulate yourself. Review the five steps of change, and write yourself a note.

As you write yourself a note about change, I want you to think of several things. What is it you want to change? What is holding you back from the change? When I left to play the game of *Survivor*, I took a sticky note and wrote myself a note. On that note I wrote, "Just Survive." I took that note and stuck it on my mirror in my closet. It was a reminder to me that I needed to survive. Even though I didn't have the note with me during the game, I took the time to write it and post it. That became a reminder to me every time I thought I couldn't survive. So, after this chapter, as you write yourself a note about change, let that note remind you daily of the change you need to make. You may need to write yourself a few notes and post one in your car, one on your board at work, and one in your wallet or purse. Wherever you need to post it, let it change you for the better, and make that change your goal. It's time to write yourself a note about a change you need to make in your life to become a better you.

Noteworthy Notes

✏️ **Kami from Florida wrote herself a note:**

"Dear Fabulous Self, do not let anyone dull your sparkle! Keep being who you are."

✏️ **Isabel from California wrote herself a note:**

"Don't let negative attitude of others affect my attitude."

Write a note to yourself about change.

_____

_____

_____

_____

_____

_____

_____

_____

_____

It is often through setbacks where we are challenged.

When you have the right mindset is when you will begin to draw from within.

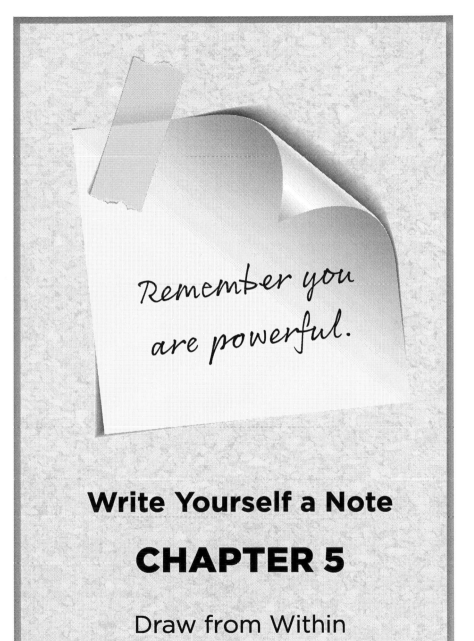

Remember you are powerful.

Write Yourself a Note

CHAPTER 5

Draw from Within

Mind over matter. For most of us, this is what we think of when we are told to draw from within. And in most situations, it is all about mindset. If you tell yourself you cannot do something, you're right. But if you tell yourself you can do something, you're probably right again. That is mindset. Mindset is, for the sake of simplicity, a belief. It is a belief about yourself and your most basic abilities. Think, for a second, about what you're good at. Think about your talents, your personality, and your intelligence. Are these traits simply fixed traits? Well, if you have a fixed mindset, you probably think that the answer is yes. People with fixed mindsets believe that their intelligence and their talents are fixed; they believe they are just inherently good at certain things and not others. Such people are stuck, because they think that they don't need to work to improve what they have. These people remain dormant for a very long time. However, when you look at these abilities as things you can develop through dedication and effort — that is when they become part of your growth mindset. If you get stuck in a fixed mindset, it does not allow for success.

Have you ever heard someone say they can't do something, because they're not smart enough or talented enough? They are stuck in a fixed mindset. However, if they changed their mindset and believed they could learn more and practice more to improve, it would allow their "growth mindset" to engage. We all have setbacks in our lives, but it is often through setbacks where we are challenged. It doesn't matter how smart, how talented, how rich or poor — we all have setbacks. But when you do have a setback, that is when you want to make sure you're not in a fixed mindset. A fixed mindset sets you up for continued disappointment. It doesn't allow you to overcome life's challenges. You need to grow to improve yourself; you need a growth mindset. With a growth mindset, you can decide to do things that can help build yourself into the person you hope to be. Stay positive. Concentrate. Work hard. Have a growth mindset. You need to work very hard on your abilities in order to succeed in life, and one of the major things having a positive, growth mindset will do for you is allow you to embrace challenges and take opportunities to reach your highest potential. A fixed mindset can stall our lives, and being "stuck" is not where most of us want to be. So, you may need to change your mindset to become a better you.

When I started speaking and traveling, I had never rented a car. I had NO idea how to even rent a car. Yes, it sounds crazy — I know! I was speaking in St. Louis, Missouri; and after talking to the meeting planner, she mentioned that I could just rent a car and drive the two hours to the location of the presentation. I was like, "WHAT? Rent a car!?" I had the wrong mindset going into this situation. The idea of renting a car was foreign to me, and I was in a fixed mindset. I told myself I could not do this, and I was not going to. My mindset was completely in the negative; I had convinced myself that I couldn't do it. Well, when I arrived at the airport, I had no idea where to go or how to rent the car. But, I decided to change my outlook and figure it out. It was the only way that I was going to get to my presentation, so I had no choice but to change my mindset. And guess what? I survived. I told myself, "You can do this. It cannot be that hard." I found the location where I needed to rent the car, I picked it up, I drove the two hours to my presentation, and I successfully returned the car. And yes, I understand that most of you are laughing right now, because this all seems so simple and easy! It's renting a car, for goodness sake! However, I had to change my mindset in order to step outside of my comfort zone and complete the task successfully. If I had remained in a negative, fixed mindset, I would have convinced myself that I was not going to rent that car. I may have talked to the meeting planner about having someone pick me up. But telling myself I could do it, and then actually doing it, allowed me to grow and learn a new skill. And now, I rent cars all the time! I know this may sound so simple that it's crazy to most of you, but it all goes back to taking opportunities and challenging yourself.

As we go back to the idea of a fixed mindset and a growth mindset, we need to explore how we go about changing our mindset. Someone who has a fixed mindset will not work hard enough to challenge himself or herself in life. But, the growth mindset is based on the idea that what we are born with is just the beginning. Where we are in life right now is just the starting point, and we can improve if we continue to work hard. So, as you move towards your ideal mindset and discover your true life's purpose, that is when you may need to change your mindset. It may seem very daunting; but once you can truly identify what you need to do on your path to a new mindset, it makes it all so much easier. Start by asking yourself, "What am I good at?" We often focus on what we aren't good at, but that won't help us to embrace our mindset and improve our lives. Make a list, right now, of all the things you're good at. Add things you love doing but maybe aren't so good at. Think about your ideal purpose above everything else in life and how the things you're good at, the things you love, and your ideal purpose can all come into alignment. That will help you to have the ideal mindset. You must love what you're doing, or it will make everything so much harder. How many people do you know are unhappy with their career? They get up every morning and complain about what time they have to be at work, who they have to work with, and what meetings they have to go to. Those people need to evaluate their "list" of what they're good at, what they love, and what their ideal purpose is. They may need to rediscover what they want to do with their lives. If you aren't happy with what you're doing, you won't have the right mindset. One of the things you can do is start looking at what you like with your job instead of focusing on what you don't like. If you truly love what you are doing, you won't even have to think about your mindset, because you will be positive and grow and learn along the way. And, my biggest advice is to surround yourself with positive people! It is inevitable that you will run into negative people who will try and take your mindset down. They will drag you down and try and break what you have accomplished. That's when you need to focus on staying on the right track. It's hard not to let negative people drag you down, and then you start believing what they are saying. But if you surround yourself with positive people and do good things, no one will be able to break your spirit.

Remember, you are powerful.

Once, I did a presentation, and I had an audience member come up to me afterwards and literally rip my presentation apart. They told me it was in the wrong order. They said I shouldn't say this, and I should talk more about that. It was very mind boggling to me; but I stood and listened, and I thanked them for their advice. But I didn't let it change my mindset. The fact is this: not everyone is going to like everything about you. But you need to remember that what you are doing in your life is touching more people in a positive way and that's what your mindset needs to focus on. We are sometimes too worried about pleasing everyone. Guess what? It's never going to happen. So, get that in your mind and realize that not everyone is going to agree with you, and you do not have to make everyone happy. As long as you have the right mindset and make yourself happy, that's what is going to keep you going.

When you have the right mindset, you will begin to draw from within. You will open up your spirit to the new you. Drawing from within will enhance your passion and help with your ability to become the improved you. As we set our minds to doing something and push ourselves beyond our limitations, we need to learn to open our spirit from within and draw from the positive. When I reached my final days of being on *Survivor*, I was extremely exhausted and it truly became mind over matter. I had to tell myself I could go on. You become very exhausted due to little or no food and hardly any rest. I am sure all of us have experienced exhaustion in one way or another. These are the times when our emotions run wild and our tempers flare up. But it truly takes the power of looking inside yourself and drawing your mindset. Find your inner spirit that tells you "Yes you can." As we competed in challenges with many nights of no sleep and very little food, it became mind over matter and drawing from within was a major asset. So, when you think you can't, think about your mindset and think about moving forward and growing. Draw positively from within; tell yourself "Yes you can."

As you write your next note to yourself, think about your mindset. Get away from your fixed mindset and go beyond. Work on your growth mindset. As we grow, we learn and improve ourselves, and that's what helps us become more successful. Write yourself a note as to how you can improve your growth mindset and become the new you.

Noteworthy Notes

 **Paula from Utah
wrote herself a note:**

"Hi, Paula. I am very proud
of you. You are stepping
out of your comfort space
and coming to this
conference, even though
you felt insecure about being
alone. I love you Paula."

 **Robin from Oregon
wrote herself a note:**

"I need to notice others and
compliment them more!"

Write yourself a note as to how you can improve your growth mindset and become the new you.

_____

_____

_____

_____

_____

_____

_____

_____

_____

_____

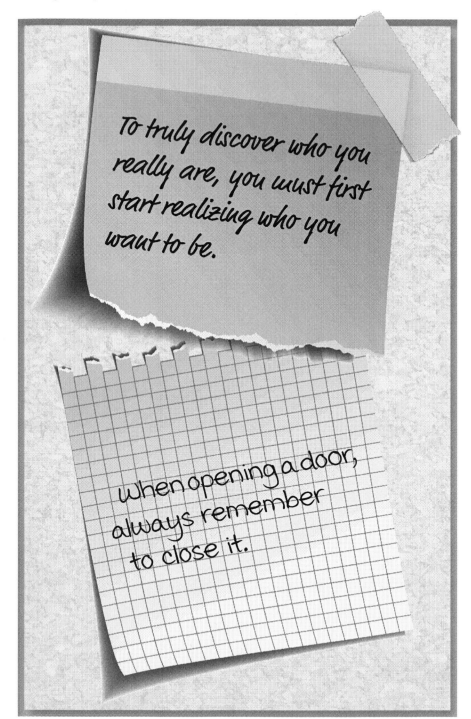

To truly discover who you really are, you must first start realizing who you want to be.

When opening a door, always remember to close it.

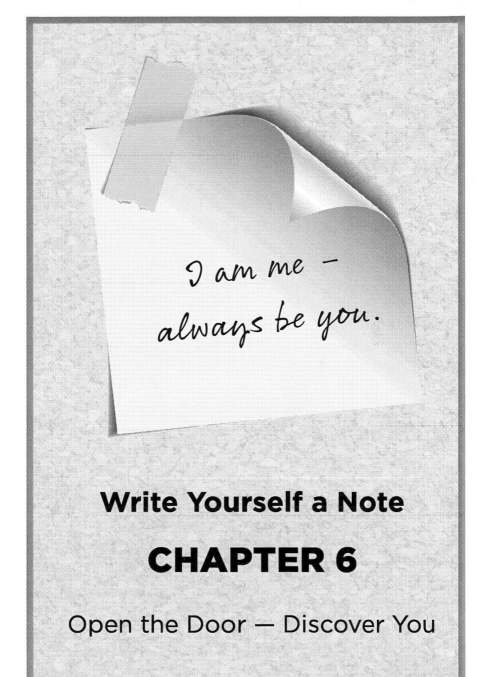

I am me —
always be you.

Write Yourself a Note

CHAPTER 6

Open the Door — Discover You

So far, we have explored the idea of taking opportunities, creating a circle, not giving up, moving forward, and changing your mindset. All of those things will open doors for you that you never thought were possible. In this chapter, I want to talk more about some of the personal issues I have had in my life and as to why I lived my life being a closed door for so long. I also want to discuss the importance of opening those doors to find your true self. However, remember that you need to realize that you are living behind a closed door before you can open it.

As a child growing up in an abusive home, it was very confusing. I could never really understand why my family wasn't like others. I always knew something was different, but I was too young to realize the real situation. I remember, as a young child, learning how to ride a bike. I never really had that much help but knew it was time to try to balance, peddle, and do it on my own. I fell many times. Sometimes, my knees were bleeding and full of scrapes and scratches; but I always seemed to get back on. As I watched other young children in the neighborhood learning to ride their bikes, their fathers were always behind them helping them to balance and pushing them along. Their fathers would let go for a short time and then grab back on to make sure they didn't fall. Their fathers would be running behind them, dripping in sweat, encouraging them along the road. Meanwhile, I always stood aside and watched how they did it to try to ride my bike by myself. I would tell myself to just keep peddling and hold on and keep the handlebars straight. I didn't have anyone holding onto the back of my bike. I didn't have anyone running with me. I had to learn that balance on my own, and I did. I can still remember the first time I went around the block by myself. At the end of the block was a big hill, and I mean a big hill, that I had to go down, and I was scared to death. The first time, I walked my bike down that hill; but on the second try, I knew I needed to do it. I made it without tipping.

As I became older, I started to realize that we did have some problems within our family. I could never have classmates overnight like my other friends did, because we never really knew how my father was going to be when he got home. As a child, I don't ever really remember my father not coming home drunk after work. After work, he would go up to the bar. As it became a habit for him, it also became an addiction. When my father became abusive, I was always scared to death. Sitting in my room as a child with the door tightly closed, praying for it to stop — the hitting, fighting, and yelling. Sometimes, I would get on my bike and ride around the block holding onto the handlebars tightly and peddling as fast as I could. Living life behind that closed door was not fun. It was a fearful challenge I had almost daily. But my bike gave me relief. As I would peddle quickly and balance with all my power, I felt in control — I felt I had power. I had learned to do this all by myself, and I could do it without falling. It was something I didn't have to do behind closed doors. It was something that I wasn't scared of.

Every time I would sit behind that closed door, on the other side were fear and the unknown. When my mother couldn't bear the abuse any longer, she made the decision to move forward. She made the decision to open that door and walk through it. She is proof that you can open a closed door and walk through it. But the important thing is that you close it behind you. Some of us walk through, but we never really close that door behind us. After my parents divorced, my father moved from town to town, and we really never knew where he was. My mother worked three jobs to raise three children, and she worked very hard. Even though my father was no longer in our home, we were still living behind that door. The abuse was gone, but the hurt and heartache was still there. We never talked about the situation or brought it up. It was something we just didn't talk about. As I took that emptiness into my teenage years, it was a struggle. I was still living behind that door but now had this huge chip on my shoulder. I was insecure, confused at times, and felt lost along the path — basically, feeling sorry for myself.

I don't have many good childhood memories because of the situation I grew up in; but that didn't give me a reason to live the rest of my life behind a closed door. For most of my life, I have struggled with having a sense of identity. Did that come from my childhood? Who are you? No, really, have you ever really considered that question? I honestly never knew who I was until I accepted the opportunity of competing on *Survivor*. That was because I had to do on my own, and there were no doors for me to hide behind. As a child, I struggled with getting on my bike and balancing. As a teenager, I struggled with knowing which friends or family members to truly trust. As a mother, I struggled with always thinking I had to do everything right. All my life, I have feared and been uncertain of who I really was until I took that one opportunity and faced fear, stepped out of my comfort zone, and started to believe in myself. I am me. I am the person who needs to get rid of the chip on my shoulder because of my childhood; I am the teenager that needs to believe in who she is and not rely on others; I am the mother who did a great job raising three amazing children. I am worthy, confident, resilient, strong, independent, successful, and smart. I am me.

Why do we have trouble saying those things about ourselves? Can you say them about you? If you can't, then you are living your life behind a closed door. Since being on *Survivor*, my life has changed. I have found out who I am but at the same time still discovering who I want to be. There have been struggles along the way, but it has made me a stronger, more independent, "I love me" person. As you reflect on who you are, think about where you are and where you want to go. So many of us get stuck. We think we have to be a certain way, act a certain way, or even be that certain someone everyone expects us to be. As we move forward in life, there are always going to be doors in front of us that we are going to have to open. But, it's how we go about opening them and also how we go about closing them.

Finding your sense of identity and opening your door is how you move forward. To truly discover who you are, you must first start realizing who you want to be. Open your door and continue to open the doors that you are faced with, because you never know when that one door will open so many others.

As you write yourself a note, think about what door in your life has been closed. It's time to open that door and walk through. Grab the handle, turn it, and move forward. Also, think about your identity, what is your identity and what do you want it to be? There are so many things to think about as you open your door; but as you open it, there will be more to open. Write yourself a note about a door you want open, and also write a note about your identity!

Noteworthy Notes

✏️ **Kate from Ohio
wrote herself a note:**

*"I'm going to be more
appreciative and grateful
for my wonderful situation."*

✏️ **Caroline from North Carolina
wrote herself a note:**

"Believe in me."

Write yourself a note about a door you want open, and also write a note about your identity!

_____

_____

_____

_____

_____

_____

_____

_____

_____

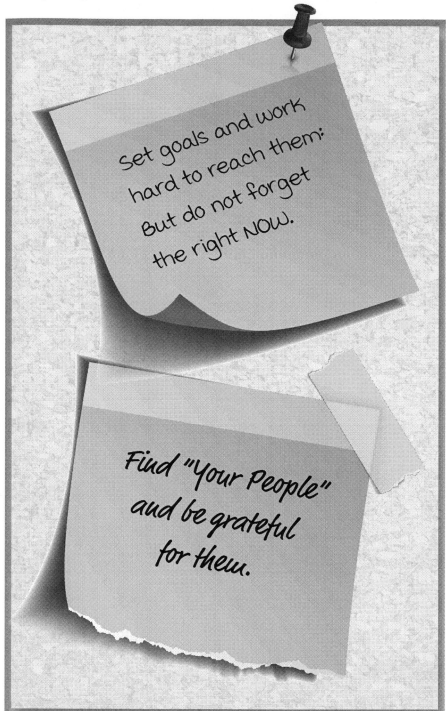

Set goals and work hard to reach them; But do not forget the right NOW.

Find "Your People" and be grateful for them.

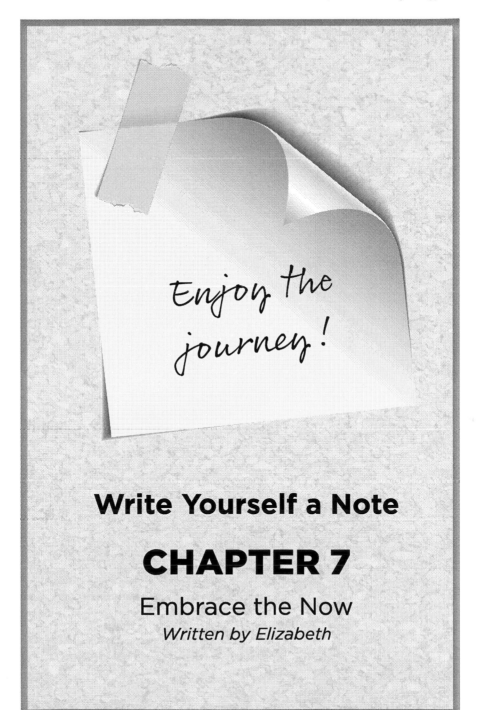

Enjoy the journey!

Write Yourself a Note

CHAPTER 7

Embrace the Now

Written by Elizabeth

(As I begin the last chapter, I have the honor and privilege to tell you that my daughter, Elizabeth, has told me that she will write the conclusion. I was beyond thrilled when she told me this! She is a bright woman with so much knowledge to share, and I have a feeling her writing her very first chapter will continue as she someday writes her own book. Have at it, Elizabeth!)

When my mother asked me to write the final chapter of this book, I was humbled. She has been a true inspiration to me and has helped me to stay motivated on my path to become a physician. She is a remarkable woman with so much insight into the tools that truly helped me to find success. I'm so incredibly proud to call her my mother and so honored that I am able to write this final chapter for her.

So far, you've learned about taking opportunities with the help of a circle of people who are there to empower you and encourage you. I have the BEST circle of people — my family, close friends, workout buddies, and colleagues.

My mother has always been one of the most important people in my circle. Her zest for life makes me want to continue to reach for my dreams. Find "your people" and be grateful for them. Life truly is about the relationships you foster with those around you.

Previous chapters have talked on the difference between giving up and moving forward and the transition to change. In college, I was extremely close to giving up my dream of becoming a physician. I was exhausted both mentally and emotionally. I did not believe that I could do it. I had to convince myself that I could move forward with my schooling. I had to change my mindset from "this is too hard" to "you can do this!"

You have also read about drawing from within and opening new doors to discover the true you. In case you didn't know, medical students go through a "match process" for their medical residency position. Essentially, you open an envelope, and it tells you where you are going to be going to finish your training as a resident physician. Opening my letter was like opening a very large and scary door. Moving from the Midwest to the Southwest was a huge change, and I had to draw a LOT of courage from within. I think I cried for the first two hours of the 14-hour car ride — with my poor newlywed husband! But I'm grateful for the experience. I'm so grateful we took the opportunity and were able to come here to finish our medical training. Oh, and the winters are MUCH, better here. Ha!

All of those things are all incredibly important, and I'd like to finish out these steps with three simple words: embrace the now.

So often in life, we focus on the past or worry about the future. However, I want you to focus on the NOW. Take opportunities, transition to change, and open doors. Keep doing all of those things! But as you're doing these things and you are taking all of the steps towards improving your life, focus on the NOW. Embrace it. You cannot change the past; it's over. And you may have a prediction about what is going to happen in the future, but it's not reality. It's an idea or an image that you have created in your head about what may or may not happen. The reality is right now. Pause for a second. Look around. Where are you? Who are you with? What sounds do you hear? Focus on the RIGHT NOW. Ignore the thoughts about what happened earlier today. Ignore the thoughts about what you have to do tomorrow. Embrace this moment right here. Now put this book down, and take ten deep breaths just focusing on the now.

You may be wondering why this is even important. Well, to make my point, I'd like to share a little bit about my journey. As briefly mentioned before, I am currently a family medicine physician finishing my residency at the University of New Mexico in Albuquerque, NM. I knew I wanted to be a doctor when I was in the fifth grade. I wanted to help people, and I thought medicine would be fun and rewarding. I studied hard in high school to maintain good grades, and I was involved in a large number of extracurricular activities in order to round out my college application. I was accepted to the University of South Dakota on a swimming scholarship, and I immediately immersed myself in Biology and Chemistry classes. However, I had an "aha" moment during my junior year of college. I realized that up until that point, I had focused so much time and energy on the end result — being a doctor. I had planned all of my classes around this goal, I had signed up for activities to help my application, I consistently thought about the future and whether or not I could do it all and actually become a doctor. I was NOT embracing the now; I was focusing on the future goal of becoming a physician. I nearly gave up on my dreams that year. I was exhausted, the classes were hard, and the schooling seemed as if it was never-ending. However, instead of changing the end goal, I just embraced the now. I changed my major. I started studying something I loved more than Biology and Chemistry. I figured I would have enough science the rest of my life, so I got a B.S. in English. I read 17th century literature. I wrote poems. I immersed myself into classes that I loved while still getting my pre-med requirements done, of course. I started focusing on the NOW. I embraced it.

I've continued that philosophy as I've continued along my journey to become a family medicine physician. I've made a promise to myself that I refuse to give up precious moments and experiences just because of a goal I've wanted to reach since the age of 11.

If I was going to go to college for four years, medical school for four years, and do three additional years to become a family medicine doctor, I was going to enjoy the journey. It would be a long eleven years of work just focusing on the end result. And I'm grateful every single day for my "aha" moment that changed my perspective.

So, my point is this: set goals and work hard to reach them, but do not forget the right now. Because you'll reach that goal, and the time it takes to get to where you want to be will pass regardless. Embrace the now. Live the now. Be the person you want to be RIGHT now. You can do it. I believe in you, and I know you can find it within yourself to believe in you too.

Noteworthy Notes

✏ **Julie from Las Vegas
wrote herself a note:**

"You are going to have a successful day."

✏ **Joan from Hawaii
wrote herself a note:**

"Believe in my strengths and abilities."

Write yourself a note about how you can focus on the now and enjoy the journey!

_____

_____

_____

_____

_____

_____

_____

_____

_____

My Notes

My Notes

_____

_____

_____

_____

_____

_____

_____

_____

_____

_____

My Notes

My Notes

Write Yourself a Note

Holly Hoffman

About the Author

Born and raised in Eureka, South Dakota, Holly Hoffman was the last remaining member of the Espada Tribe and the last woman standing on Season 21 of CBS' hit reality show *Survivor Nicaragua*. Through that experience, and others throughout her life, Holly was inspired to share her message of positivity, determination, and confidence with business leaders, teachers, and students across the nation.

A professional speaker and the author of both *Write Yourself a Note* and *Your Winner Within*, Holly acknowledges that life is made up of challenges, and we are oftentimes faced with situations that seem insurmountable. But within each of us is an ability to focus our thoughts, emotions, and energy to succeed — if only we have the knowledge, tools, and discipline to do so.

Holly Hoffman

PROFESSIONAL SPEAKER & AUTHOR

HollyHoffman.org

Faith. Attitude. Determination. Confidence. Desire. Perseverance.